T0087577

PLAY BALLADS
With A Band

Music Minus One

3841

SUGGESTIONS FOR USING THIS MMO EDITION

WE HAVE TRIED to create a product that will provide you an easy way to learn and perform these compositions with a full ensemble in the comfort of your own home. The following MMO features and techniques will help you maximize the effectiveness of the MMO practice and performance system:

Because it involves a fixed accompaniment performance, there is an inherent lack of flexibility in tempo. We have observed generally accepted tempi, and always in the originally intended key, but some may wish to perform at a different tempo, or to slow down or speed up the accompaniment for practice purposes; or to alter the piece to a more comfortable key. You can purchase from MMO specialized CD players & recorders which allow variable speed while maintaining proper pitch, and vice versa. This is an indispensable tool for the serious musician and you may wish to look into purchasing this useful piece of equipment for full enjoyment of all your MMO editions.

We want to provide you with the most useful practice and performance accompaniments possible. If you have any suggestions for improving the MMO system, please feel free to contact us. You can reach us by e-mail at *info@musicminusone.com*.

Music Minus One

3841

contents

TRUMPET

WITCHCRAFT

Carolyn Leigh and Cy Coleman
Arranged by Bob Wilber

TRUMPET SOLO - (MELODY)

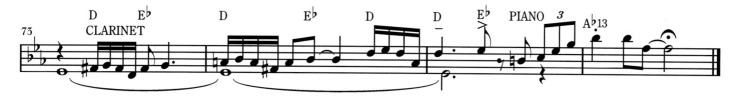

TRUMPET

ONE FOR MY BABY
(And One More For The Road)

Johnny Mercer and Harold Arlen
Arranged by Bob Wilber

8

TRUMPET

TENDERLY

Jack Lawrence and Walter Gross
Arranged by Bob Wilber

MMO 3841

TRUMPET

THE CHRISTMAS SONG
(Chestnuts Roasting On An Open Fire)

Mel Torme and Robert Wells
Arranged by Bob Wilber

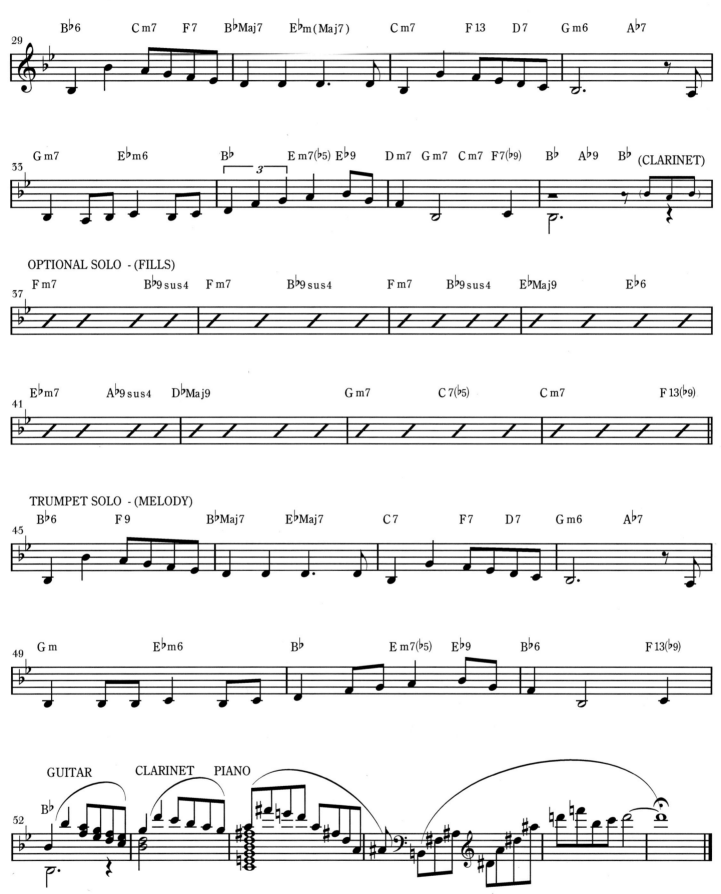

TRUMPET

AFTER YOU'VE GONE

Henry Creamer and Turner Layton
Arranged by Bob Wilber

TROMBONE SOLO

8

TRUMPET

MANHATTAN

Richard Rodgers and Lorenz Hart
Arranged by Bob Wilber

TRUMPET

WHY DON'T YOU DO RIGHT

Joe McCoy
Arranged by Bob Wilber

TRUMPET SOLO-
(MELODY)

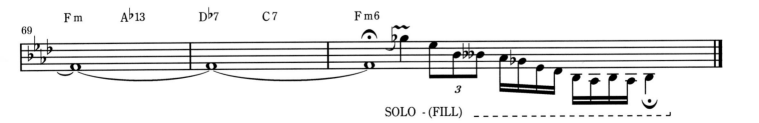

TRUMPET

I'M GLAD THERE IS YOU

Paul Madeira and Jimmy Dorsey
Arranged by Bob Wilber

TRUMPET

WHAT A DIFF'RENCE A DAY MADE

Stanley Adams and Maria Grever
Arranged by Bob Wilber

TRUMPET

SENTIMENTAL JOURNEY

Bud Green, Les Brown and Ben Homer
Arranged by Bob Wilber

MUSIC MINUS ONE
50 Executive Boulevard
Elmsford, New York 10523-1325
800-669-7464 (U.S.)/914-592-1188 (International)

www.musicminusone.com
e-mail: info@musicminusone.com